Bible reflections
for older people

BRF

The Bible Reading Fellowship
15 The Chambers, Vineyard
Abingdon OX14 3FE
brf.org.uk

The Bible Reading Fellowship (BRF) is a Registered Charity (233280)

ISBN 978 1 80039 040 9

Acknowledgements
Scripture quotations marked with the following abbreviations are taken from the version shown. Where no abbreviation is given, the quotation is taken from the same version as the headline reference. NIV: The Holy Bible, New International Version (Anglicised edition) copyright © 1979, 1984, 2011 by Biblica. Used by permission of Hodder & Stoughton Publishers, a Hachette UK company. All rights reserved. 'NIV' is a registered trademark of Biblica. UK trademark number 1448790. NLT: The Holy Bible, New Living Translation, copyright © 1996, 2004, 2007, 2013. Used by permission of Tyndale House Publishers, Inc., Carol Stream, Illinois 60188. All rights reserved. CEV: The Contemporary English Version. New Testament © American Bible Society 1991, 1992, 1995. Old Testament © American Bible Society 1995. Anglicisations © British & Foreign Bible Society 1996. Used by permission. NEB: The New English Bible – Oxford University Press, Cambridge University Press, 1970. – © The Delegates of the Oxford University Press and the Syndics of the Cambridge University Press 1961/1970. NKJV: The New King James Version®. Copyright © 1982 by Thomas Nelson. Used by permission. All rights reserved. NRSV: The New Revised Standard Version of the Bible, Anglicised edition, copyright © 1989, 1995 by the Division of Christian Education of the National Council of the Churches of Christ in the United States of America. Used by permission. All rights reserved. TLB: The Living Bible copyright © 1971 by Tyndale House Foundation. Used by permission of Tyndale House Publishers Inc., Carol Stream, Illinois 60188. All rights reserved. MSG: *The Message*, copyright © 1993, 1994, 1995, 1996, 2000, 2001, 2002 by Eugene H. Peterson. Used by permission of NavPress. All rights reserved. Represented by Tyndale House Publishers, Inc.

Every effort has been made to trace and contact copyright owners for material used in this resource. We apologise for any inadvertent omissions or errors, and would ask those concerned to contact us so that full acknowledgement can be made in the future.

A catalogue record for this book is available from the British Library

Printed and bound in the UK by Zenith Media NP4 0DQ

Contents

About the writers

Martyn Payne worked with BRF for over twelve years before his retirement in 2017. His last role was Messy Church researcher, and he has a background in Bible storytelling and leading all-age worship and is passionate about the blessing that comes when generations explore faith together. His BRF books include *Messy Parables* (2017), *Creative Ways to Tell a Bible Story* (2013) and *Where in the World?* (2012).

Lin Ball's career began in journalism over 40 years ago. She delights in the variety of work that has come her way: ghost-written books, magazine articles about missionary work, communications for Christian charities and radio interviews on disability. Lin lives in the East Midlands, where she still writes, is active in eco-groups and enjoys long walks.

David Butterfield was successful in the 2017 writing competition for readers of *The Upper Room* Bible reading notes. After studying music, he felt the call to ordination in the Church of England. During his 40-year ministry, he served at churches in Southport, the Midlands and Shropshire. His final post was at York Minster, from which he retired in 2017. He and his wife Irene now live in Ripon in North Yorkshire.

Ro Willoughby has been writing and editing Christian resources for many years. She has recently been licensed as a lay minister at St Chad's Woodseats in Sheffield, where she is engaged in ministry with people of all ages. It is a great joy that she now lives close to her children and grandchildren as well as close to Bakewell and Chatsworth House!

From the Editor

Welcome to this new collection of Bible reflections.

I have a lovely friend called Kavita. Her name means 'poem' and, by destiny or design, she is a gifted poet as well as an award-winning novelist.

The invitation to Kavita's 50th birthday party came with a request to guests to send her their favourite word and her promise that she would create a poem out of all our words. Sure enough, some months later, a unique, intriguing poem arrived. As with all the best poems, it has a beauty and resonance far greater than the sum of its parts.

Poetry was an unlikely casualty of last year's lockdown when the exam regulator Ofqual made it optional for GCSE English students, in order to free up timetable space for supposedly more important subjects.

I am grateful and honoured that the poet Ann Lewin is a regular contributor to *Bible Reflections*. As a former English teacher herself, I can only imagine her dismay that, had pupils actually been able to sit their exams, they could have been awarded their GCSE English Literature qualification without studying a single poem. Kate Clanchy is another poet, writer and teacher who is passionate about encouraging her students to write their own poetry. A vocal critic of Ofqual's decision, she argued: 'Poetry needs to be central, not an option.' This is why, right at the centre of every issue of *Bible Reflections*, there is a poem. I hope you enjoy them.

God bless you.

Using these reflections

Perhaps you have always had a special daily time for reading the Bible and praying. But now, as you grow older, you are finding it more difficult to keep to a regular pattern or find it hard to concentrate. Or maybe you've never done this before. Whatever your situation, these Bible reflections aim to help you take a few moments to read God's word and pray, whenever you have time or feel that would be helpful.

When to read them

You may find it helpful to use these Bible reflections in the morning or last thing at night, but they work at any time of the day you choose. There are 40 reflections here, grouped around four themes. Each one includes some verses from the Bible, a reflection to help you in your own thinking about God, and a prayer suggestion. The reflections aren't dated, so it doesn't matter if you don't want to read every day. The Bible verses are printed, but if you'd like to read from your own Bible that's fine too.

How to read them

- **Take time** to quieten yourself, becoming aware of God's presence, asking him to speak to you through the Bible and the reflection.

- **Read** the Bible verses and the reflection:
  - What do you especially like or find helpful in these verses?
  - What might God be saying to you through this reading?
  - Is there something to pray about or thank God for?

- **Pray**. Each reflection includes a prayer suggestion. You might like to pray for yourself or take the opportunity to think about and pray for others.

Another way of seeing

Martyn Payne

For me, losing track of my glasses has become an all-too-normal part of life as I have grown older. I am forever hunting them down to be able to read. However, even though enabling good eyesight is vital, there is more to seeing than meets the eye – if you'll pardon the wordplay.

Seeing is more than receiving an image with the lens of our eyes. The stories of the Bible point us to another way of seeing, which is about discerning God's invisible presence and recognising God's signature on the things that happen to us every day. The apostle Paul calls this way of seeing 'faith' – he writes 'we live by faith, not by sight' (2 Corinthians 5:7, NIV).

Jesus began his ministry at the synagogue in Nazareth, where he read from the book of Isaiah with its prophecy about someone who would bring, among other things, 'recovery of sight for the blind'. Jesus came to help us see properly; to see ourselves, each other and God, as each truly is. This sort of seeing is at the heart of our Christian discipleship, and the following Bible reflections aim to explore and nurture this other way of seeing.

Now where *did* I put my glasses?

Luke 4:20b–22 (NIV)

Blind eyes

The eyes of everyone in the synagogue were fastened on [Jesus]. He began by saying to them, 'Today this scripture is fulfilled in your hearing.' All spoke well of him and were amazed at the gracious words that came from his lips. 'Isn't this Joseph's son?' they asked.

I'm sure you'll have had the experience of looking for something for ages and, just when you're about to give up, there it is, right in front of you. How could you have missed it? You just couldn't see for looking, as we say.

That synagogue morning at Nazareth ended dramatically. One moment the congregation were amazed and couldn't take their eyes off Jesus; the next they hounded him out of town wanting to kill him. Here's a good example of seeing, but not seeing. The congregation had seen Jesus deliver a stunning reading, announcing himself as Messiah; but Jesus was hoping they'd seen something more; he was longing to 'see' faith. But all they could say was, 'Isn't this the carpenter's son?'

Jesus then used two stories to provoke them into recognising who he was and what God is like, but they didn't get it; and as the mob swept him up the hill, Jesus disappeared. They didn't see him anymore. Their blindness became their downfall, not his.

I wonder what we don't see because we're only seeing what we want to see, not what is really there. We need the Holy Spirit to help us see afresh.

■ **PRAYER**

'Open our eyes, Lord, we want to see Jesus.' Amen

Luke 8:10 (NIV)

Closed eyes

[Jesus] said, 'The knowledge of the secrets of the kingdom of God has been given to you, but to others I speak in parables, so that, "though seeing, they may not see; though hearing, they may not understand."'

Everybody loves a story. Stories can ignite the imagination and draw people in more than a straightforward talk, because stories can help us see things in a whole new way. I wonder if any stories have done this for you recently.

Jesus's favoured teaching method was to use stories, or parables, as we know them. Superficially they can seem simple, but within are layers of meaning for those who have eyes to see. When Jesus told the parable of the sower, for example, his disciples suspected that there was more to the story than met the eye; and Jesus confirmed that they were on the right track, quoting from Isaiah: 'though seeing, they may not see'.

Parables are designed to provoke us into taking a second look and dis-covering deeper truths. For example, Jesus helped his friends see that the parable was not so much about the sower or the seed, but about the soil; he changed the focus as he explained it. But note, he helped them because they asked. Because they had begun to recognise their blindness, they wanted to know how to look and Jesus enabled them to see.

■ **PRAYER**
Help me, Lord, to recognise my blindness and let you open my eyes. Amen

Psalm 115:4–5 (NIV)

Blind idols

Their idols are silver and gold, made by human hands. They have mouths, but cannot speak, eyes, but cannot see.

I wonder if you have ever had to sew an eye back on to a much-loved teddy bear belonging to a young relative. Such artificial eyes can look quite real, but of course they aren't. They can't really see like we can, or think we can.

In this psalm, the writer sings of the foolishness of those who make an idol. Such handmade gods have eyes but they are sightless. They can't look with love on us like the living God. Similar verses occur elsewhere in the Bible. Isaiah 44:9–20 describes at length the carving of a log into a god to worship, calling it madness. It just reveals our own blindness. We may think we see ourselves and our world properly; we may imagine we understand who we are and what God is like – but in reality we are blind to so much. We must recognise that blindness as the first step to a true, open-eyed life with God.

There is so much that we don't see in the moment. We all need the sightedness that comes through faith in God to find our way through life each day.

■ **PRAYER**

Lord, open the eyes of our hearts to see the world and people, as you do. Amen

Ephesians 1:18 (NIV)

The eyes of the heart

I pray that the eyes of your heart may be enlightened in order that you may know the hope to which he has called you, the riches of his glorious inheritance in his holy people.

Parents and teachers, it's said, need to have 'eyes in the back of their heads' when caring for active, and possibly mischievous, children. Who knows what they may be up to behind your back?

In a similarly figurative way, the apostle Paul writes about 'the eyes of your heart', which need to be opened to see the hidden things of God. This idea of an inner eye is found in many religions, along with teachings about how we can find enlightenment. But this isn't what Paul is talking about. His inner eye is an eye that only God can open. This same teaching is there in Jesus' words (Luke 11:33–36) when he says this eye is like an internal lamp. Jesus calls it the 'eye of the body', but it's something more than our physical eyes. It's the inner me and you – our soul or spirit – which when lit up can help us see properly.

We need God to turn this light on, as we believe in him. The alternative is darkness… a spiritual blindness. Both Paul and Jesus urge us to see with these eyes, so we can be filled with God's light.

■ PRAYER
Open the eyes of our hearts, Lord, and fill us with your light. Amen

Luke 6:41 (NIV)

Sawdust and planks

[Jesus said,] 'Why do you look at the speck of sawdust in your brother's eye and pay no attention to the plank in your own eye?'

Getting something in our eye can be really irritating and even painful. Our eyes water and we just can't see clearly. It's a temporary form of blindness we all might experience at some time in our lives. This is the background to this well-known saying by Jesus.

It comes after he has described some spiritual teachers as 'the blind leading the blind'; they both end up falling into a pit. His criticism of the religious leaders of his day is uncompromising; it's no wonder it made him unpopular. But Jesus goes on to apply the truth to all of us, again with exaggerated humour, talking about someone having a plank in their eye, not just some annoying speck of dust! Clearly people must deal with their own blindness first, before trying to open other people's eyes. Jesus isn't only saying 'don't judge others' but also 'face up to your own need for Christ to give you light'.

We all tend to be quick to see the faults of others, but we need to remember that we all have our blind spots, particularly concerning ourselves. As we come close to God today in prayer, let's ask the Holy Spirit to put that right.

■ PRAYER

Lord, first heal my own blinded sight, before I can with compassion reach out to help others. Amen

Mark 8:25 (NIV)

Seeing slowly

Once more Jesus put his hands on the man's eyes. Then his eyes were opened, his sight was restored, and he saw everything clearly.

Touch is an important and sometimes undervalued sense. A hug, an arm on our shoulder or a squeeze of the hand can mean such a lot and bring comfort and healing to us. I wonder how important touch is to you.

The touch of Jesus was already well recognised as a way to experience healing. Think of how the woman in the crowd only had to touch the hem of his garment. Touch can take human connection to another level, saying more than words, adding depth to listening and going beyond merely seeing the other person. And of course, touch was the language this blind man most understood. His friends wanted Jesus to touch him, but note how Jesus gave so much more. He gently led the man by the hand to a less public place and then touched his eyes more than once, restoring his sight, slowly and lovingly.

Each of us is unique, and coming to see Jesus clearly will take as long as it needs to take in the hands of the one who touches us with patient love. How might you pass on this touch of love and healing today, helping others to see Jesus?

■ PRAYER
Thank you, dear God, for your touch of love on my life that is helping me slowly but surely to see you more clearly. Amen

1 Samuel 16:7 (NIV)

Seeing the heart

'The Lord does not look at the things people look at. People look at the outward appearance, but the Lord looks at the heart.'

In his fairy story *The Princess and Curdie*, the Christian writer George MacDonald describes how Curdie can recognise a creature's true nature by taking its hand in his own. Honest people have human hands, but those with evil intentions have hands that feel like hooves and claws. We all know that people aren't always what they appear to be on the outside. We need the gift of seeing beyond the surface of things.

Even the 'see-er' Samuel had to learn from God how to see properly. One of Jesse's sons was to be anointed king, but which one? They all looked strong, handsome and up to the job. Even David is described as healthy and good-looking. Samuel had to learn how to see a person's heart. This seeing showed him that it was the youngest son, David, who would be 'a man after [God's] own heart' (Acts 13:22).

Only God can give us this gift of seeing which goes deeper than what we take in with our naked eye. God wants us to ask for this spiritual sight, so that we can see others and what's happening in our world today, as God sees them.

■ **PRAYER**
Help me, Lord, to see people, day-to-day situations and the world around me with your eyes. Amen

2 Kings 6:17 (NIV)

Opening eyes

Elisha prayed, 'Open his eyes, Lord, so that he may see.' Then the Lord opened the servant's eyes, and he looked and saw the hills full of horses and chariots of fire all round Elisha.

The Bible's stories of receiving sight aren't just about people who were once physically blind. Sighted people need to have their vision restored too. Just as we say to someone, 'You just can't see for looking,' we can miss what is staring us in the face.

When God opens eyes, we begin to see heaven all around us. In the story of Elisha and his servant, the enemy's moves are known in advance by Israel because, by the gift of God, Elisha is able to see into the enemy camp. But later, when the king of Aram sends an army to kill Elisha, the prophet's servant can only see the enemy – an overwhelming and menacing force. So Elisha prays for his servant's eyes to be opened. Here is a sighted person being healed of his blindness, a blindness to the heavenly dimension all around him. When he looks again, he sees the far superior angel armies surrounding those who surrounded them. They are in safe hands because God is there.

I wonder how many unseen angels there are about us right now, protecting, encouraging, praying with and inspiring us in God's name.

■ PRAYER
Lord, open your servants' eyes to see your protecting presence that surrounds us every day. Amen

Mark 10:51b–52 (NIV)

Unseen Bartimaeus

The blind man said, 'Rabbi, I want to see.' 'Go,' said Jesus, 'your faith has healed you.' Immediately he received his sight and followed Jesus along the road.

I wonder if you've ever experienced the frustration of calling out to a friend across a crowded shopping precinct, only for your cry to be lost in the general hustle and bustle. We live in a generally very noisy world these days, and it's so easy not to be heard or even seen.

In today's story, though unusually we do have a name for the blind man, we only know his surname ('son of Timaeus'). In other words, people didn't use his first name. Maybe no one had ever bothered to find it out. No wonder Bartimaeus shouted out loud: he was used to being overlooked, used to people walking on by and not seeing the one who couldn't see. This story begins with the crowd's blindness as much as Bartimaeus'.

But where the crowd didn't really want to see Bartimaeus or respond to his shouting, Jesus saw and heard faith. He responded to the heart behind the cry. Maybe we too can sometimes fail to notice people like this, and we need to have our eyes opened to really see the people in need who surround us every day.

■ **PRAYER**
Lord, help me to see those invisible people in need who I might so easily walk past this day. Amen

2 Corinthians 4:18 (NIV)

Faith opens eyes

So we fix our eyes not on what is seen, but on what is unseen, since what is seen is temporary, but what is unseen is eternal.

As we've discovered from our Bible readings on this theme, we often get it wrong when it comes to seeing and not seeing. In everyday speech, we glibly respond with the words 'I see', when really we don't see at all. True seeing is much deeper than what our eyes see. We need faith to see properly.

This contrast between faith and seeing is one which comes out strongly in Paul's writings. It's been suggested that Paul's eyesight wasn't good – maybe he never quite recovered from that blinding light on the Damascus Road – and for that reason he particularly understands about walking not by eyesight but with the eyes of faith. Elsewhere, Paul reminds us that here we see 'as in a glass darkly'. What we think we see isn't everything.

Faith is the way into this new seeing. With eyes of faith, we can reassess our circumstances not as hopeless but as opportunities to receive grace. With eyes of faith, we can reassess people not as lost causes but as souls for whom Christ died. With eyes of faith, we can reassess the sights and sounds of creation not as cosmic accidents but as gifts of God for us to enjoy.

■ PRAYER

Father God, help us to walk more and more by faith and not by sight. Amen

In praise of clouds

Lin Ball

Cumulus… stratus… cirrus… stratocumulus… altocumulus… nimbo-stratus… cirrocumulus… More than 100 types of clouds exist, grouped into ten basic types, depending on their shape and how high they are in the sky. Each cloud is made of floating water drops or (the higher ones) ice crystals, and is a vital part of the earth's weather patterns.

I wonder why clouds have such a bad press. Someone 'under a cloud' is in a bad mood, in disgrace or perhaps suspicious. Someone with their 'head in the clouds' is impractical, unrealistic. Yet clouds have a particular beauty, and I love how their changes reflect the weather.

As older people, we don't have the monopoly on changeable circum-stances. But at times, it can feel as if we have diminishing control over them, particularly when illness or disability affects our independence.

The changing clouds in the sky remind us of life's many contrasts. A permanently blue sky would soon lose its appeal. The radiant rain-bow would be less striking without the backdrop of clouds. Perhaps our joy in the good times in our lives would be reduced without challenging clouds to provide contrast.

Job 37:15–16 (NLT)

He moves the clouds

'Do you know how God controls the storm and causes the lightning to flash from his clouds? Do you understand how he moves the clouds with wonderful perfection and skill?'

The constantly changing distribution of clouds above the earth is a fascinating feature of the view from space. We hardly give clouds a second thought, except perhaps to get our umbrellas out when they darken. Yet a moment's reflection will remind us how varied they are in shape and texture, and how lovely.

Though we seldom think about them, clouds are hugely important in regulating our weather patterns and global temperatures. Sometimes they cool the earth by reflecting the sun's energy; sometimes warm it by acting as an energy-trapping blanket. They are a key part of the creator's design. The landscape of living plants and animals needs daily water to flourish.

Today's verses come from an amazing exchange between Job, his 'comforters' and the Lord himself as they debate the majesty of creation. Dip into Job 36:26—39:30 to feel over-awed by the wonder of all God has made.

■ **PRAYER**

Look up at the sky, if you are able, as you pray: Lord, your clouds that float and gather, your storehouses of snow, your torrents of rain and rushing winds, your life-giving sun… All sing your praises, great God of creation. And I, too, made by your hand, I praise you. Amen

Proverbs 8:27–29 (CEV, abridged)

He placed the clouds

I was there when the Lord put the heavens in place and stretched the sky over the surface of the sea... when he placed the clouds in the sky and created the springs that fill the ocean... when he set boundaries for the sea to make it obey him, and when he laid foundations to support the earth.

In this psalm, the voice is that of 'Wisdom' – one of the great attributes of the creator God.

As we reflect on the beauty, balance, variety and interconnectedness of the created world, it's a small step to consider all that generations have done to throw the natural world into imbalance and confusion, demonstrating the very opposite of wisdom. Thousands of animal and plant species are lost every year. We have induced catastrophic climate change by our thoughtlessness and greed.

Clouds are God's provision of vital water, appearing in the sky in very small droplets, so light that they float. The joining of droplets creates rain or hail or snowflakes – part of a complex global system for irrigation superior to anything manmade. Our meddling with nature has led to droughts, floods and heat-waves, resulting in impoverishment of the most vulnerable peoples of the world.

■ PRAYER
Forgive your people, Lord God, for the terrible damage we have done to all the nurturing natural systems you put in place to benefit us. Help me to do what I can to care for your creation. Amen

Psalm 97:1–2, 4–5a (NIV)

Majesty and mystery

The Lord reigns, let the earth be glad; let the distant shores rejoice. Clouds and thick darkness surround him; righteousness and justice are the foundation of his throne... His lightning lights up the world; the earth sees and trembles. The mountains melt like wax before the Lord.

Did you know that there is a Cloud Appreciation Society? New members receive a cloud selector wheel to help them identify the 20 most common cloud formations. Perhaps an appreciation of clouds can lead to an appreciation of the cloud creator?

There are many references in the Bible to God's throne being surrounded by clouds. The image speaks not just of majesty but of mystery. We talk of 'cloud cover'. Clouds shield, hide and disguise. The Bible suggests that the beauty of the Lord would be too intense to be seen in its totality, that clouds protect us from his full glory.

In Exodus 40:35 we read, 'Moses could not enter the tent of meeting because the cloud had settled on it, and the glory of the Lord filled the tabernacle.' Sometimes we become too casual about our faith. Has the cloud from around God's throne melted away for you?

■ PRAYER

Majestic God, help me to consider afresh how great you are and how much you love me. Fill me with wonder and praise. Renew my faith and my relationship with you. Amen

Lamentations 3:41–42, 44 (NIV)

Covered with cloud

Let us lift up our hearts and our hands to God in heaven, and say: 'We have sinned and rebelled and you have not forgiven... You have covered yourself with a cloud so that no prayer can get through.'

Jeremiah is the only Old Testament writer to have witnessed the fall of Jerusalem, and that's one of the reasons he's thought to be the writer of Lamentations. This book grieves the destruction of the beloved city, expressing deep sadness and emotional pain for the dreadful outcome, which is attributed to the unfaithfulness of God's people.

The haunting lyric of these poems is that living our own way brings sorrow and despair. Since God is sovereign and just, 'Why should the living complain when punished for their sins?' the poet calls out (3:39). The people are urged to repent and return to God.

Have you experienced an apparently deaf God? When we call on God from an unrepentant heart, our voice is 'clouded' – hidden from him. Check to see if the cloud that obscures him has been put in place by you, rather than him.

■ PRAYER

'Return to the Lord your God, for he is gracious and compassionate, slow to anger and abounding in love,' says another prophet (Joel 2:13). If you feel your prayers aren't reaching God, that he is shrouded in cloud, search your heart. Say sorry if you need to – and claim Joel's promise.

Exodus 13:21–22 (NIV)

Through the wilderness

By day the Lord went ahead of them in a pillar of cloud to guide them on their way and by night in a pillar of fire to give them light, so that they could travel by day or night. Neither the pillar of cloud by day nor the pillar of fire by night left its place in front of the people.

The story of the exodus – the miraculous delivery of God's people from slavery – is rich in vibrant pictures which can symbolise a personal journey with God. The burning bush that set Moses on his path as leader, the awful plagues sent to the Egyptians, the Passover lamb and blood on the door lintels, the crossing of the Red Sea – these events easily take on allegorical meaning for us.

Why didn't the pillar of fire burn 24/7? We can't answer that question, of course. But I wonder if God chooses to guide through the clouds of life – dark, grey times when we can't see ahead – just as often as through fires – dramatic times of revelation and action.

When there's no drama, no excitement, it's harder to believe God is in control. But trusting on cloudy days is vital.

■ **PRAYER**

'Through all the changing scenes of life, in trouble and in joy, the praises of my God shall still my heart and tongue employ,' wrote 17th-century hymn writers Nahum Tate and Nicholas Brady. Help me to know that as a daily reality, Father. Amen

1 Kings 18:43–44a (NIV)

Small as a person's hand

'Go and look toward the sea,' [Elijah] told his servant. And he went up and looked. 'There is nothing there,' he said. Seven times Elijah said, 'Go back.' The seventh time the servant reported, 'A cloud as small as a man's hand is rising from the sea.'

In this story, God shows his power by putting an end to drought and famine through the persistent prayers of Elijah. The first glimmer of an answer was small… as small as a man's hand. But then 'the sky grew black with clouds, the wind rose, a heavy rain came on…' (v. 45).

Persistence is an underrated virtue, and persistence in prayer an undervalued discipline.

Why was the cloud 'as small as a man's hand'? Perhaps it's because Elijah needs to know that a person's capacity is infinitesimal compared to the almighty God who controls the seasons and the climate. Perhaps persistence in prayer is easier when we come to the realisation that we have and are nothing, that all the power is his.

And take a look at Elijah's great faith (v. 44b) at the news of that tiny cloud.

■ **PRAYER**

Father, my faith is as small as that cloud. Help me to persist in prayer for the people and the causes that are close to your great heart. Amen

Ecclesiastes 11:4, 6 (NLT)

Planting under the clouds

Farmers who wait for perfect weather never plant. If they watch every cloud, they never harvest... Plant your seed in the morning and keep busy all afternoon, for you don't know if profit will come from one activity or another – or maybe both.

I was in my mid 30s before I took an international flight. Taking off from Heathrow on a bitterly cold January day with scattered snow on the ground, I well remember the moment when the plane broke through the canopy of grey clouds – above which the sky was brilliant blue and the sun was shining. Somehow, I had never fully appreciated that the sun is always there above the clouds, and that clouds bathed in sunshine look completely different from above than when viewed from below.

It's all a matter of perspective. If we wait for perfect conditions before we act, then we will live a paralysed life. If we wait for the perfect opportunity before we speak out for Jesus, or tell someone we love that God loves them, perhaps we will be sentencing ourselves to a life of silence. If not now, when?

Our task is to sow the seeds, even on cloudy days. It's the Lord who prospers them.

■ **PRAYER**
Lord, show me if I am letting clouds be a barrier to action. I am imperfect, and my circumstances and opportunities are imperfect – but I am perfectly available to you. Amen

Jude 1:12–13 (NLT)

Clouds with no rain

When these people eat with you in your fellowship meals com-memorating the Lord's love, they are like dangerous reefs that can shipwreck you. They are like shameless shepherds who care only for themselves. They are like clouds blowing over the land without giving any rain. They are like trees in autumn that are doubly dead, for they bear no fruit and have been pulled up by the roots. They are like wild waves of the sea, churning up the foam of their shameful deeds. They are like wandering stars, doomed forever to blackest darkness.

The short but hard-hitting letter of Jude was written to warn believers about teachers of false doctrine. Wrong teaching, he says, promises much but gives nothing, just like clouds which produce no rain.

Is it because we believe ourselves to be an educated and sophisticated society that we rarely consider ourselves to be threatened by false teaching? Yet if you watch TV, read a daily paper or have a Facebook page, the chances are you are exposed to anti-biblical philosophies and lifestyle choices every day. We are bombarded by secular thought patterns, such as extravagant consumerism, which promise personal fulfilment but distract us from holy living – and ultimately are clouds with no rain.

■ PRAYER

Are you sensitive to the ungodly teaching you are exposed to in your daily life? How can you counter this and focus on absorbing godly wisdom instead? Talk to God about any changes you may need to make.

Genesis 9:12–14 (NLT)

Rainbow in the clouds

Then God said, 'I am giving you a sign of my covenant with you and with all living creatures, for all generations to come. I have placed my rainbow in the clouds. It is the sign of my covenant with you and with all the earth. When I send clouds over the earth, the rainbow will appear in the clouds.'

The influential American writer Maya Angelou wrote, 'Try to be a rainbow in someone's cloud.'

Despite their beauty, despite how essential they are to the balance of the world's weather patterns, often the word 'cloud' is synonymous with darkness or sadness. Let's admit it: we all have dark times in our lives. Yet without clouds, there can be no rainbow. And a rainbow is rather more distinctive and beautiful against the backdrop of a stormy sky than a cloudless one.

'*When* I send clouds,' says our Bible verse. We don't like to think of God sending sadness into our lives, but can we say that he is sovereign and not believe that all our experiences are sent by him? The clouds that herald the rainbow are part of the enriching contrasts of life. Blue skies every day would lose their attraction eventually.

■ PRAYER

Summon up any dark places in your life and name them before God. Then, hard as it may be, ask God to teach you through them. And, yes, dare to ask him for rainbows.

Matthew 24:30–31 (NLT, abridged)

The clouds of heaven

And then at last... they will see the Son of Man coming on the clouds of heaven with power and great glory. And he will send out his angels with the mighty blast of a trumpet, and they will gather his chosen ones from all over the world – from the farthest ends of the earth and heaven.

Whether this is allegorical or actual, it's wonderful to think that the most significant clouds we might ever see could be the clouds carrying Jesus as he returns to earth, rescuing his people to reign with him on the renewed earth. After a period of great turbulence, writes Matthew, quoting the Old Testament prophets Isaiah and Daniel, the skies will be the scene of extraordinary happenings heralding the arrival of the King of kings – the climax of history at a time only known to his Father.

I write this on a stormy afternoon with a blue sky scattered with billowy cumulonimbus, giant grey and white cotton balls producing intermittent fierce showers with the possibility of rainbows. The Met Office describes cumulonimbus as 'the king of clouds... extending high into the sky in towers or plumes'. Perhaps the glorious Jesus, who once entered Jerusalem on a humble donkey, will return from heaven to earth on just such a majestic cloud. Come, Lord Jesus!

■ PRAYER

As I look into the skies, may the beauty of your clouds, Father God, remind me of the coming return of your Son, our Saviour Jesus. And may I be ready, be waiting, for that hour. Amen

The Gift of Years

 Debbie Thrower is the pioneer of BRF's Anna Chaplaincy for Older People ministry, offering spiritual care to older people, and is widely involved in training and advocacy.

Visit **annachaplaincy.org.uk** to find out more.

Debbie writes…

Summertime. Don't we all remember as children rolling sideways down grassy hills, landing dizzy and disorientated, lying on our backs looking up at the clouds, seeing shapes in their ever-changing forms? We must remind ourselves, sometimes, to just enjoy the landscape.

One nature writer recommends bending over to see a view through one's legs, framed upside down. I don't know how agile you are still! But I see her point. Viewing the world upside-down improves one's powers of observation, shocks our senses into seeing things anew. It's what each of our writers is doing in this edition.

I've been reading *Cloud Atlas* by David Mitchell. In the final pages the hero pledges himself to cultivating belief: 'Belief is both prize and battlefield… Why? Because… if we *believe* that humanity may transcend tooth and claw, if we *believe* diverse races and creeds can share this world… peaceably… only as you gasp your dying breath shall you understand, your life amounted to no more than one drop in a limitless ocean! Yet what is any ocean but a multitude of drops?'*

I hope you enjoy reflecting on God, and your part in creation, in all sorts of fresh ways.

Best wishes

Debbie

* Hodder and Stoughton, 2004, pp. 528–29.

Meet the writer: Martyn Payne

 We're delighted to welcome Martyn Payne. Before retiring in 2017, he was the Messy Church researcher for BRF. He has a background in Bible storytelling and leading all-age worship and is passionate about the blessing that comes when generations explore faith together. Martyn trained as a teacher in London and spent 18 years teaching languages and RE. He then spent eight years with the Church Mission Society as its national children's work coordinator before joining BRF in 2002. Early last autumn he took on the leadership of a small – 'tiny' – church in an Essex village on the outskirts of London. His BRF books include *A-cross the World* (2004), *Where in the World?* (2012), *Creative Ways to Tell a Bible Story* (2013) and *Messy Parables* (2017). He told us how he first came to faith:

'I reluctantly joined confirmation class at school, but it didn't really mean anything to me and I got confirmed not really knowing what I was doing. But it did mean having to go to church, meeting Christians and being drawn into a youth group where there were some wonderful leaders who nurtured me and shared the gospel with me. I came to faith there in my late teens. And I met my wife there, Ruth, so we've been together a long time.'

What brought him to BRF?

'I joined BRF in 2002 to help develop Barnabas in Schools. It was new for me in various ways, not least because I began working in primary schools. And, in fact, I've actually enjoyed primary school work even more than secondary school.

'I found trying to communicate what Christians believe in a way that was thought-provoking and fun and engaging for young children very challenging, but in a really good way. It was also groundbreaking because it was about working alongside schools where they were, not storming in and telling them what they should be doing and believing.

'At first I was working with Lucy Moore, who went on to pioneer Messy Church in 2004. But after ten years of wonderful but demanding work with Barnabas in Schools, in 2012 I reached 60 and it was time to rethink. Messy Church had got to the stage where they were looking to grow their team and they invited me to join them. So for the next five years I was called the Messy Church Researcher. Research sounds a bit boring, but it wasn't at all. It was people-meeting, listening work and travelling all over the country, coming alongside people and often taking part in Messy Church sessions.

'I do love traditional worship, but I'm very conscious that when you have a family in which two or three generations might have had no experience of church, you need another way in: a way that tells the same story but in a creative participative way. That's what Messy Church does and I've seen it work incredibly effectively. It doesn't always, of course, but done well, it's brilliant, and I've been to more Messy Churches that have been amazing than have been disappointing. And they are church, I would argue. I believe in it strongly.'

Why is storytelling so important to Martyn?

'When I first became a Christian, a lot of it was about getting the doctrine right and being taught well, and I understand all that. But as I've got older, I've been drawn more and more to the gospels. When you read the gospels, you see how Jesus taught, and it was through stories. So I began to explore storytelling. I actually pray, "Lord, help me to be a storyteller," because being a good storyteller doesn't necessarily come naturally. It can be a natural gift, but even then, like all gifts, we need God's grace to help the gift grow.

'Story works on so many levels. A story can hold people of different ages, different abilities, different interests, backgrounds, cultures… If you set out to try to teach something specific, to get a particular point over, it can be very hard to connect with different people. You've got to get the language right, to know what their past experience is, to understand their culture – but stories just draw people in.

'I think sometimes the church worries that we're "just" telling stories. We're not teaching people properly how to be disciples. But I think that's rubbish: stories can take you very deep into discipleship. I've seen it happen.

'As we get older, story is more and more important. Grandparents tell stories. I remember my grandparents telling me stories, and I remember my dad telling my children stories. Stories are a great connector across the generations. It's like when you're climbing a hill and turn round and see where you've come from – seeing the path that has brought you to where you are now.

And intergenerational worship?

'I'm so passionate about this, and so much research backs this up. We need peer groups, of course, but for wholeness of being we need to connect with all ages. This is one of the reasons Messy Church works so well. Traditional churches are sometimes more multigenerational than intergenerational. There might be different age groups but they're not actually mixing together.

What for Martyn is 'the gift of years'?

'I find I look forward to, and am more daring about, the opportunity to be playful. It was George Bernard Shaw who said, "We don't stop playing because we grow old; we grow old because we stop playing."

'I find myself being happier to play, and to just try things, and to be a bit more daring at times. It's about being more childlike as I get older. I wrote a prayer about this, called "When I grow up":'

I want to be a child when I grow up.
I want to go on asking questions, exploring mysteries and keep on playing.
I want to go on laughing, wondering and embracing the moment.
I want to be a child when I grow up.

Katie Norman and Messy Vintage

Katie was born on Jersey and has spent all but a few years of her life on the island. Unusually, her whole family lives there too: her husband, two daughters, and two grandchildren. She's a local preacher in the Methodist Church, but her main passion is being a team leader for both Messy Church and Messy Vintage. Rheumatoid arthritis limits Katie's mobility, but she's adventurous and energetic and makes full use of a special walker which enables her – punctures notwithstanding – to go beach-combing and cliff-climbing. Katie came up with the idea for Messy Vintage over ten years ago and is thrilled with how it has flourished. She's also very excited about the newly-published book *Messy Vintage*, written with Jill Phipps. We are asked Katie to tell us more.

'Messy Vintage is for those who prefer a slightly slower pace of life and those for whom perhaps a traditional church is not something they can cope with any more. It's aimed mainly at people who are slightly older or those with additional needs. It has developed and grown and it's a wonderful blessing not only for the people who come, but the team too: it's just wonderful.'

Now with the book, it's going to get out to a much wider audience still...

'Yes, it's really exciting. As with the original idea, I just felt that this was something God really wanted to happen, because it's so very important that our older folk not only have the opportunity to share in some form of Christian service, but are also able to participate at whatever level they can manage. For some people, that might only be pointing to a colour, but still you see their eyes light up. Some people may not be able to sing or play an instrument, but they may be able to tap their foot. It really is engaging with people where they are and respecting them completely. It's not about controlling the environment; it's about allowing something to happen, and it really is very inspiring.'

If you had one wish for this book, what would it be?

'My co-author, Jill Phipps, and I hope that we've been able to convey, through the one-dimensional black-and-white words on the page, the beauty and the value of being able to offer a spiritual experience to people in a very different way. For people who are already doing this kind of work, they'll be able to dip in and out of the book and hopefully discover lots of new ideas. But for people who haven't encountered this approach before, we hope it will be a huge eye-opener, and that it will inspire them to offer Messy Vintage in all sorts of different communities. The need is there in all communities: rural, urban and everywhere in between.

'My desire is that we've been able to convey that to people who have a heart for ministry to the older generation, and that it will just trigger something in them. I'm confident that once they take that tentative first step, and begin to offer Messy Vintage within their communities, the work will just flourish. You have to be very adaptable and accept that things won't always – will maybe never – go exactly according to plan, but it is incredibly worthwhile and a blessing for everyone involved.'

For more information about Messy Vintage, see **messychurch.org.uk/messyvintage**.

For more information about *Messy Vintage: 52 sessions to share Christ-centred fun and fellowship with the older generation*, go to **brfonline.org.uk**.

Pilgrimage

 Ann Lewin has written several series for *Bible Reflections for Older People*, but she is best known as a poet, and particularly for her much-loved collection *Watching for the Kingfisher* (Canterbury Press, 2009). Reflecting on her experience of last year's long months of lockdown, Ann writes:

'Suddenly the landscape of life had no signposts, just a boundary that required me to stay indoors except for necessary outings. I wasn't in the shielding category, but am in my 80s, old enough for people to offer to do my shopping for me, a kindness I was very grateful for. I'm used to living on my own and am happy in my own company. I have a well-established pattern to my days, based on the Benedictine concept of a balance between work, rest, prayer and recreation. I wasn't going to lack something to do in my spare time, but it was odd not knowing what would happen or how long it would take for this virus to be dealt with.

'Early on, I realised that it would be important not to lose hope. I made a poster that said "Let hope keep you joyful" to put in my window, to encourage passers-by, as well as myself, to remember to work at it. Hope for Christians is based on remembering that God's faithfulness is constant. Whatever happens, God will be with us, and that is a real cause for thankfulness. Joy is not the same as cheerfulness; it is much deeper, springing from thankfulness for God's unfailing love. When I had moments of wondering if we would get through this, I remembered that God will never let us down, and we need not be afraid.'

Ann's poem, 'Pilgrimage to Llandecwyn', is from *Waiting for the King-fisher*. It describes St Tecwyn's Church, high on the hills between Porthmadog and Harlech. It captures the Christian's enduring hope, and also echoes the theme of meeting God in high places, which Ro Willoughby explores in the pages that follow.

Pilgrimage to Llandecwyn

*Prayer has soaked into this
Place for centuries.
Gravestones leaning in the wind
Bear witness to generations
Who have trodden the lanes
Before us. And still
A presence holds, enfolds and
Challenges all who come.*

*Light glances on changing
Patterns in the estuary,
Reflecting angels' wings
As they come bringing
The world's needs for attention,
And return bearing peace
To the troubled world.
The waters catch fire
With the glory of God
In the setting sun.*

*Inside the church,
Simplicity.
Silence deepens, the only sound
The heartbeat of the place,
Heartbeat of God.*

Favourite hymns

David Butterfield

In 2013, viewers of the BBC's *Songs of Praise* were invited to vote on their favourite hymns. Thousands of people responded, and the most popular 100 hymns were listed. In this series of reflections, I have chosen ten hymns from that list for us to think about.

As a musician, I have always enjoyed singing hymns and songs, and I enjoy the best of old and new. When we ask people why they like a particular hymn, I find that they often point to the tune. However, when we take a moment to examine the words of hymns, we discover that they are a gold mine of spiritual truth, as I hope we will find.

There's not enough space to include all the words of the hymns in these reflections. You may possibly know the words of these well-loved hymns by heart. But if you don't, and don't already own a hymn book, might you be able to borrow one, so that you can read through the words of each hymn along with the reflection.

I wonder which is your favourite hymn – and why?

Psalm 103:1–2 (NIV)

'Praise, my soul, the king of heaven'

Praise the Lord, my soul; all my inmost being, praise his holy name. Praise the Lord, my soul, and forget not all his benefits.

Do you ever talk to yourself? I confess that I do when there's no one else in the house. I'm reassured by the fact that King David, who wrote this psalm, talked to himself. He begins the psalm by saying, 'Praise the Lord, my soul.' In 1834, those words inspired Henry Francis Lyte to write this hymn, though he had to change the word order of the first line to make it scan.

I don't always feel like praising the Lord, and I imagine that may be true of you. That's why it's good to praise God as an act of will – as a habit – because he is always worthy of our praise, no matter how we feel. I find that when I do that as an act of will, my feelings often follow, as I am drawn into worship and prayer.

In the psalm, King David reminds himself of the benefits that God has blessed him with. So why not take a moment to think of the reasons why it would be fitting for you to praise the Lord? Then have a word with yourself and say, 'Praise the Lord, my soul.'

■ PRAYER

Thank you, O God, that you are always worthy of praise. Help me praise you no matter how I am feeling, knowing that you are slow to chide and swift to bless. Amen

Psalm 104:24 (NIV)

'All things bright and beautiful'

How many are your works, Lord! In wisdom you made them all; the earth is full of your creatures.

It was in 1848, at the age of 30, that Cecil Frances Alexander wrote a collection of 24 hymns for little children, with each one based on a line of the creed. Three remain very popular to this day. This hymn is based on the phrase 'I believe in God, the maker of heaven and earth.'

My wife Irene and I enjoy walking, and it's a blessing to live in North Yorkshire, which is a beautiful part of the world. When we go for a walk, I'm aware that Irene often notices the beauty of creation more than I do. She might point to the different colours of lichen and moss growing on a fallen tree or the colour and shapes of various wild flowers.

It's good to reflect on the beauty and complexity of creation, to see God's fingerprints and to respond with wonder and say, in the words of the hymn, 'How great is God almighty who has made all things well.' I wonder which aspects of creation inspire in you a sense of awe and wonder. Take a moment to thank God for the beauty of his handiwork and creativity.

■ PRAYER

O Lord, give me eyes to appreciate more and more the beauty of the world you have made, so that I may tell how great is God almighty, who has made all things well. Amen

Ephesians 2:8–9 (NIV)

'Amazing grace'

For it is by grace you have been saved, through faith – and this is not from yourselves, it is the gift of God – not by works, so that no one can boast.

John Newton was a slave trader. In 1748, a violent storm battered his ship so severely that he called out to God for mercy. This moment marked his spiritual awakening and he later abandoned his life as a slave trader and devoted his life to serving God, being ordained into the Church of England in 1764. He became popular as a preacher and hymn writer, penning some 280 hymns. Among them, 'Amazing grace' must be the best known.

The meaning of the word 'grace' is the undeserved generosity of God that he shows us when he forgives us and gives us new life in Christ. John Newton was so conscious of not deserving anything good from God that he uses the word 'grace' six times in the first three verses of the hymn.

We can sometimes picture God as a 'headmaster figure' rather than a loving heavenly Father. Yet the picture of God that Jesus gives us is one of him searching for us with love. As we look back over our lives, we can probably all think of things we wish we had not done. The hymn 'Amazing grace' encourages us to receive God's love and forgiveness afresh as a free gift today.

■ PRAYER

Heavenly Father, thank you that your grace has brought me safe thus far. Help me to live each day with an awareness of your love for me and your grace. Amen

Philippians 4:6–7 (NIV)

'Dear Lord and Father of mankind'

Do not be anxious about anything, but in every situation, by prayer and petition, with thanksgiving, present your requests to God. And the peace of God, which transcends all understanding, will guard your hearts and your minds in Christ Jesus.

Before I retired, my wife and I lived in York for three years. When friends came to visit us, we would often take them for a walk around the walls. They are a reminder of the days of past conflict when the people of York needed to guard themselves against attack so that they could live in peace.

All these years later, there are many things that can rob us of a sense of inner peace. It can be illness, anxiety about the future, worry about people we love and so many other situations. In his letter to the Christians at Philippi, Paul encourages us to bring our worries to God in prayer. When we do this, he says that God's peace will 'guard' our hearts. So, like the walls around the city of York, God's peace can protect us from those anxieties that can rob us of a sense of calmness and serenity. Instead, in the words of John Greenleaf Whittier, the writer of this hymn, we can pray for 'the beauty of thy peace'.

If there are particular cares and concerns that are robbing you of your peace today, give them to God in prayer and ask that his peace will guard your heart.

■ PRAYER
Heavenly Father, drop thy still dews of quietness till all my strivings cease. Take from my soul the strain and stress, and let my ordered life confess the beauty of thy peace. Amen

Luke 1:46b–47 (NEB)

'Tell out, my soul, the greatness of the Lord'

'Tell out, my soul, the greatness of the Lord, rejoice, rejoice, my spirit, in God my saviour.'

In 1961, the Revd Timothy Dudley-Smith acquired a copy of the recently published *New English Bible*. Turning to Luke 2, he read the first line of the Magnificat and it inspired him to write this well-known hymn.

In one section of her song of praise, Mary recalls how our God is a God of justice who 'has filled the hungry with good things but has sent the rich away empty'. We are all too aware of the injustices in our world where so many people suffer from a lack of the basic necessities of life, while others bask in luxury. It's easy to shrug our shoulders and assume that there is little that can be done about it.

However, there are many relief agencies (including the faith-based Tearfund and Christian Aid) through which substantial numbers of people do receive much needed help. As George Hoffman, the founder of Tearfund, said, 'One person cannot change the world, but you can change the world for one person.'

You may already support such a relief agency financially and in your prayers. If not, could this be something you might consider doing? In this way, we can all play our part in seeing 'the hungry fed, and the humble lifted high'.

■ PRAYER

Heavenly Father, may those who are hungry today be fed. May the humble be lifted high. Amen

Revelation 4:8b (NIV)

'Holy, holy, holy, Lord God Almighty'

'Holy, holy, holy is the Lord God Almighty, who was, and is, and is to come.'

If we were to ask a young child, 'Why do you love your Mummy?', the child might say, 'Because she cooks me my favourite meal,' or 'Because she reads me bedtime stories.' If we then were to say, 'I know someone who cooks fantastic meals and tells wonderful bedtime stories, so would it be okay for this person to do this for you instead of your Mum?', the child would almost certainly reply, 'No!' Although a young child would be unable to articulate why someone else wouldn't do, we know it's because children love their parents for who they are, not just because of what they do for them.

It's the same with our relationship with God. We often praise and thank God for what he does for us. However, when we worship and adore him for who he is, there is a step change in our worship. This is the sort of worship we see in heaven as the heavenly beings praise the one 'who was, and is, and is to come'.

As you reflect on this hymn, written by Reginald Heber, spend a few minutes offering God your worship and adoration for who he is.

■ PRAYER

Holy, holy, holy, Lord God Almighty, God in three persons, blessed Trinity, I worship and adore you. Amen

Malachi 1:11 (NIV, abridged)

'The day thou gavest, Lord, is ended'

'My name will be great among the nations, from where the sun rises to where it sets...' says the Lord Almighty.

You have probably seen the photograph of the earth taken on 7 December 1972 by the crew of the Apollo 17 spacecraft on its way to the moon. It's called 'Blue Marble' and is one of the most reproduced images in history.

As we think of the earth continually turning and some people going to sleep and others waking, it reminds us of how at all times there are people somewhere on earth praising God. This is the thought that dominates this hymn, written by John Ellerton in 1870. It's captured particularly in verse three in his poetic phrase, 'The voice of prayer is never silent, nor dies the strain of praise away.'

So when we pray, we can be encouraged that we belong to a world-wide body of people, and at all times there are always some who are praising God somewhere on earth. In your prayers today, you could pray for any people you know in other countries of the world who at this moment may be sleeping or waking, or working or praying.

■ PRAYER

Heavenly Father, we thank thee that thy church, unsleeping, through all the world her watch is keeping, and rests not now by day or night. Amen

Luke 24:28b–29 (NKJV)

'Abide with me'

Then [the two disciples and Jesus] drew near to the village where they were going, and He indicated that He would have gone farther. But they constrained Him, saying, 'Abide with us, for it is toward evening, and the day is far spent.' And He went in to stay with them.

It was in 1927 that the first and last verses of this hymn were sung for the first time at a FA Cup Final. It was a game between Arsenal and Cardiff City. This tradition has continued to this day. It would be interesting to know why this particular hymn was adopted in this way by football supporters.

'Abide with me' was written in 1847 by Henry Francis Lyte, who also wrote our first hymn, 'Praise, my soul, the King of heaven'. At the time he was a very sick man. He died three months later. 'Abide with me' speaks of the quiet confidence that Christians can have as we draw to the end of our lives. The hymn is a prayer asking the Lord to abide with us – to stay with us. Henry Lyte contrasts how 'the world and its desire are passing away, but those who do the will of God live forever' (1 John 2:17, NRSV).

So may we share the confidence of the author of this hymn, that when our faith is firmly in Christ, we can look forward with a quiet confidence to the day when for us 'heaven's morning breaks and earth's vain shadows flee'.

■ PRAYER

In life, in death, O Lord, abide with me. Amen

Matthew 28:1–3 (NIV)

'Thine be the glory, risen, conquering Son'

After the Sabbath, at dawn on the first day of the week, Mary Magdalene and the other Mary went to look at the tomb. There was a violent earthquake, for an angel of the Lord came down from heaven and, going to the tomb, rolled back the stone and sat on it. His appearance was like lightning, and his clothes were white as snow.

This hymn, 'À toi la gloire', was written in French by the Swiss hymn-writer Edmond Budry in 1885 and later was translated into English. We sing it to the rousing tune composed by Handel. In 1977, my wife and I chose it for our wedding service. It recounts the amazing story of how on that first Easter morning, an angel 'in bright raiment rolled the stone away'.

Down the years, some people have attempted to disprove the resurrection of Christ. However, if he didn't rise from the dead, why didn't the Jewish authorities produce the body which had been guarded by soldiers? And why were so many followers of Jesus willing to give their lives for what would have been a lie?

With its focus on the truth of the resurrection of Christ, this hymn reminds us that our faith is not some mystical experience based on wishful thinking, but is based on historical facts that Jesus lived, died for our sins and rose again. May this fill us with confidence and joy as we sing, 'Thine be the glory!'

■ PRAYER

Lord Jesus Christ, I pray for those people I know who are sceptical about the facts of Easter. Open their eyes so that they might meet you, risen from the tomb. Amen

Philippians 2:10–11 (TLB)

'At the name of Jesus'

At the name of Jesus every knee shall bow in heaven and on earth and under the earth, and every tongue shall confess that Jesus Christ is Lord, to the glory of God the Father.

The author of this hymn, Caroline Noel, spent the last 25 years of her life bedridden due to a painful and crippling illness. Rather than allow this to get her down, she composed verse, and, among a collection published in 1871, was 'At the name of Jesus'.

As those of us who are older look back over our lives, we are aware of how many things have improved in amazing ways. We think of huge leaps forward in the areas of medicine, communications and transport, to name but a few. At the same time, we are all too aware of distressing and persistent problems: injustice, inequality, conflict and ecological crisis. At times, we may wonder what the world is coming to.

This hymn gives us hope as it looks forward to the day when 'Jesus will return again, with his Father's glory and his angel train'. It will be a day when, in the words of the writer of the book of Revelation, 'There will be no more death or mourning or crying or pain' (Revelation 21:4, NIV).

May this hymn encourage you and give you hope as you look forward to the day when the rule of God will be fully established.

■ PRAYER

Lord Jesus Christ, thank you that you are ever to be worshipped, trusted and adored. Thank you that when we trust in you, our future is secure. Come, Lord Jesus. Amen

Come, climb with me

Ro Willoughby

Our bodies are made for climbing. You may have marvelled at toddlers who fearlessly clamber over a climbing frame. As a child, you may have climbed trees or used ropes in the school gym. You may have lived halfway up a hill or in a block of flats without a lift. Maybe you climbed mountains on holiday, or loved driving in a mountainous area, climbing steep hills then pausing to appreciate the view. Everything looks different from above.

Over my life I have been a climber in a variety of ways and places, although these days my knees complain at very steep gradients. I am inviting you to come climbing with me. I hope my experiences will remind you of the role that climbing has played in your life.

There are many mountains and hills in the Bible. We shall visit some of them, as well as a tall building and a tree. We will find God in every place that we climb. My prayer is that as you come climbing, you will encounter God there and be strengthened and refreshed in your relationship with him. After all, God is so great – higher than the heavens (Job 22:12).

Psalm 95:3–6a (NIV)

View from the top

For the Lord is the great God, the great King above all gods. In his hand are the depths of the earth, and the mountain peaks belong to him. The sea is his, for he made it, and his hands formed the dry land. Come let us bow down in worship.

My friends who live in the South Lake District wanted to show me their favourite view. They kept describing it to me in terms of 'breathtaking on a good day'. We went up the road, skirted the working quarry, then climbed to the highest point. This was a clear day. The panoramic view was stunning – south-east over Morecambe Bay, as far as Blackpool Tower and north up to the high mountains of the Lake District, west over the Duddon estuary. But I felt very small.

This mountain belongs to God, just as the quarry does. For decades it has provided stone for communities. The sea is God's too, literally stretching as far as the eye can see. It was like a coastal map laid out before me. Here was detailed beauty. Here was evidence of God's power in creation.

These timeless verses come from what's called the Venite, Psalm 95. I used to sing this as a child every Sunday morning. God calls us to worship him.

■ **PRAYER**

Picture in your mind a panoramic view that thrilled you. Praise God for his beautiful world, but also remember that, as insignificant as you may feel, you matter to him.

Psalm 24:1, 3–4 (NIV)

Pilgrim climbers

The earth is the Lord's, and everything in it, the world, and all who live in it... Who may ascend the mountain of the Lord? Who may stand in his holy place? The one who has clean hands and a pure heart, who does not trust in an idol or swear by a false god.

Recently I walked the Peak Pilgrimage, a 37-mile route that calls by 14 churches. It took me four days. In the beautiful Peak District there are many steep climbs. One afternoon, we laboured up the steep hill from the River Dove to the village church of Alstonefield. This church provides all pilgrims with refreshments and a peaceful place for rest and prayer.

I was reminded of the pilgrims who climbed up the hill to worship God in Jerusalem, singing these verses. The psalm may have been composed by King David for the momentous return of the ark of the covenant to Jerusalem. The ark was the physical representation of God, the king of glory. Anyone who intended to stand in God's holy place needed to be clean in God's eyes, determined to remain faithful to him.

We are pilgrims and God travels along with us. We come respectfully and honestly into his presence. We ask for cleansing from sin. We seek his help to be faithful.

■ PRAYER
David wrote, 'Create in me a pure heart, O God, and renew a steadfast spirit within me' (Psalm 51:10). Pray this before you speak with God today.

Psalm 18:1–2; Proverbs 18:10 (NIV)

Climb to safety

I love you, Lord, my strength. The Lord is my rock, my fortress and my deliverer; my God is my rock, in whom I take refuge, my shield and the horn of my salvation, my stronghold... The name of the Lord is a fortified tower; the righteous run to it and are safe.

It was a challenge for a class of eleven-year-olds to climb to the top of St Paul's Cathedral. The view from the top made it worthwhile. Then the fire alarm went off. Of course, we had to descend as quickly as possible. But as I endeavoured to keep children moving but calm, I wondered if, since this was probably a false alarm, we'd have been quite safe remaining at the top of the brick structure.

The citadel of Jerusalem, like most medieval castles, was built on a hill. Castles were places where people could run when threatened by an enemy. In a medieval castle, once the drawbridge was pulled up, people were safer. In the Old Testament, God is often described as a tower of refuge. It is a powerful image. When we feel weak, insecure or afraid, God calls us to come to him to find safety. What is your experience of 'fleeing' towards God for protection?

■ **PRAYER**

Slowly read these Bible verses as you pray. If you feel anxious or afraid, picture yourself protected in a strong castle, with the drawbridge pulled up. No danger can reach you. God is your refuge.

Psalm 121:1–2, 7–8 (NIV, abridged)

A place of fear

I lift up my eyes to the mountains – where does my help come from? My help comes from the Lord, the Maker of heaven and earth... The Lord will... watch over your life; the Lord will watch over your coming and going, now and forevermore.

Most of the climbing done in this series has been in the hope of meeting God. However, mountains can be frightening places. Once, we climbed Snowdon confident that it was a good day for climbing. But, near the top a mist enveloped us. We were lost. No fantastic views. Just fear. Eventually we found the path that led to safety – no need to call the mountain rescue.

The mountains in this psalm would not help anyone meet God. In the Old Testament, people sometimes built altars to false gods in high places. They looked to the hills to offer sacrifices to the Baals. 'Don't look to the mountains,' writes the psalmist. 'Instead, you must look to the Lord, who made heaven and earth.' We don't worship the creation, but the creator, the only living God, and we can worship him anywhere.

When we were lost on Snowdon, we cried out to God to rescue us. He heard our cry. He always does. He goes with us, knowing our every movement.

■ PRAYER

Whether or not you feel lost or fearful, remember that God knows where you are and is with you. Thank him that we are never out of his sight.

Exodus 19:16–20 (NIV, abridged)

Keep on climbing

There was thunder and lightning, with a thick cloud over the mountain, and a very loud trumpet blast... Moses led the people out of the camp to meet with God, and they stood at the foot of the mountain. Mount Sinai was covered with smoke, because the Lord descended on it in fire... The Lord... called Moses to the top of the mountain.

The day I climbed Ben Nevis, the highest mountain in Great Britain, was hot. The path up was like rush-hour. Halfway up, I felt exhausted. I couldn't go on. But my friend was determined we should get to the top. We rested, and I drank some water and ate something. We set off again. Refreshed, my energy and determination had returned.

Moses needs strength and determination to hear from God and receive the ten commandments. He never gives up. Once at the top, God instructs him to go back to warn everyone to stay away from the mountain. It is holy ground. Moses climbs up again. He is there so long that the people persuade Aaron to build a golden idol. When Moses finally comes down, he destroys the stone tablets in anger. He has to go up, yet again.

■ **PRAYER**

Sometimes it seems like hard work to keep going with God. We may not want to climb the mountains before us, whatever they are, but God calls us to come, just as he did Moses. Ask him to help you today to persevere in your journey with him.

1 Kings 19:11–13 (NIV, abridged)

A mountain retreat

A great and powerful wind tore the mountains apart... After the wind there was an earthquake... After the earthquake came a fire, but the Lord was not in [any of them]. And after the fire came a gentle whisper. When Elijah heard it, he pulled his cloak over his face and went out and stood at the mouth of the cave. Then [God's] voice said to him, 'What are you doing here, Elijah?'

Ffald y Brenin is a beautiful retreat centre in the hills of Pembrokeshire. It is a centre for prayer and a place where people meet God. One Easter, exhausted from the demands of work, we retreated there – and were refreshed.

In this passage, Elijah has directly challenged the evil intentions of King Ahab, Queen Jezebel and hundreds of false prophets. In the power of God, he has miraculously defeated them. But the effort has left him utterly empty. He runs away and, after being given food and water by an angel, he reaches the mountain called Horeb. It is here, in the almost-silence, that God listens to Elijah's fears and loneliness and then sends him on his way on another mission.

■ PRAYER

You may be feeling weary, frustrated and alone, or you may be facing a difficult situation which makes you afraid or anxious. Tell God how you feel, knowing that just as God knew what a state Elijah was in, he also knows about you. He will give you the strength you need. Elijah did not expect God to meet him in quietness.

Isaiah 40:29–31 (NIV)

View from the sky

He gives strength to the weary and increases the power of the weak. Even youths grow tired and weary, and young men stumble and fall; but those who hope in the Lord will renew their strength. They will soar on wings like eagles; they will run and not grow weary, they will walk and not be faint.

The sun was setting. Flying to Switzerland with a window seat, I saw several snow-capped mountain peaks rising above the thick, fluffy, white clouds. The peaks were pink! I had to fly high to catch this stunning, never-to-be-forgotten view. Do airline pilots ever tire of the view?

Eagles occur throughout the Bible, known for fiercely protecting their young and also as a symbol of strength and courage. When God rescued his people from Egypt, he is described as protectively 'carrying them on eagle's wings' to bring them to himself.

Centuries later, the people of Israel were trapped and dispirited in exile in Babylon. These words from the prophet Isaiah could reassure them. Like eagles, they would be strong and full of energy. Like eagles, they could look down from above and trust that God knew what he was doing.

What is the highest point on this planet you have ever reached? Imagine you are an eagle looking down on your life. Where can you see God being present with you?

■ PRAYER

Ask God to help you 'hope in the Lord', to keep you safe and to give you strength for this day.

Matthew 14:22–23 (NIV)

Go up to pray alone

Immediately Jesus made the disciples get into the boat and go on ahead of him to the other side, while he dismissed the crowd. After he had dismissed them, he went up on a mountainside by himself to pray. Later that night, he was there alone.

In the Peak District there are some amazing cliff edges, where the rock has fallen away to leave a sharp drop. These edges are great for serious climbers who use ropes. They are also great places to walk, with fantastic views. When I want to be alone for a serious conversation with God, I walk along Baslow Edge. Usually there are few people around. Walking helps me concentrate as well as admire the view and wildlife.

Jesus goes up the mountain to be alone with his Father. It is night, so he probably doesn't walk around. He needs this space and time. We don't know what is said. But he isn't cutting himself off from the needs of those he loves, because at some point he realises his disciples are in trouble on the lake. He goes to rescue them.

We don't need to climb a mountain to meet with God. But we do need to find a space where we can be still in his presence. That makes it possible for us to re-enter our everyday lives to help those in need.

■ **PRAYER**

Amidst all the clatter of daily living, 'Be still, and know that I am God.'

Matthew 17:1–3, 5 (NIV, abridged)

Meet God at the top

Jesus took with him Peter, James and John the brother of James, and led them up a high mountain by themselves. There he was transfigured before them. His face shone like the sun, and his clothes became white as the light. Just then there appeared Moses and Elijah, talking with Jesus... A bright cloud covered them, and a voice from the cloud said, 'This is my Son, whom I love; with him I am well-pleased. Listen to him!'

During the coronavirus pandemic, I moved in with my daughter and family. For three months I stayed in their attic with a large skylight. Every evening after our meal, I climbed the stairs to my eyrie at the top of the house. Here I had time and space to read, reflect and talk with God. Several times God took me by surprise.

Peter, James and John could not have anticipated what would happen when Jesus took them up the mountain. They 'met' Moses and Elijah and saw Jesus in an utterly different light. They heard God declare Jesus as his Son. They couldn't make sense of it, but they would never forget it. Jesus told them not to speak about this experience until after his resurrection. Only then do they understand.

Some people do experience God's presence up a mountain. But we can meet God in high places or on ground level, indoors or in the open, and in the depths of the earth or the sea.

■ PRAYER

When did God last surprise you with words he has said or something you discovered about him for the first time? Ask God to continue to surprise you again and again.

Luke 19:2–5 (NIV)

Climb to hide away

A man was there by the name of Zacchaeus; he was a chief tax collector and was wealthy. He wanted to see who Jesus was, but because he was short he could not see over the crowd. So he ran ahead and climbed a sycamore-fig tree to see him, since Jesus was coming that way. When Jesus reached the spot, he looked up and said to him, 'Zacchaeus, come down immediately. I must stay at your house today.'

I'm not a tree-climber, but in the Royal Botanic Gardens at Kew, in London, there is a treetop walkway. After climbing up several flights of steps, it is possible to walk high above the trees, noticing the birds, and, unseen, to gaze down on everything below.

Zacchaeus is determined to see Jesus. Being so short, he needs to climb a tree to get a good view of this famous preacher. The *ficus sycomorus*, still common in Israel, is tall, with long spreading branches and thick foliage. By climbing this tree, Zacchaeus is not only hidden from the crowd, who dislike him, but, unnoticed, can observe Jesus.

But Jesus knows his name and knows he is hiding. He wants a private conversation with Zacchaeus because, along with his family, he matters to Jesus. His life is transformed by Jesus spending time with him.

■ PRAYER

'Is there anyplace I can go… to be out of your sight? If I climb to the sky, you're there!… You're already there waiting' (Psalm 139:7–10, MSG). Picture yourself climbing to a high place to hide, but Jesus is there already, welcoming you by name. What will you say to him?

God at work in the ordinary every day, from one generation to the next...

*Hear, O Israel: The Lord our God, the Lord is one... These command-
ments that I give you today are to be on your hearts. Impress them on
your children. Talk about them when you sit at home and when you
walk along the road, when you lie down and when you get up.*

DEUTERONOMY 6:4–7 (NIV, abridged)

Two things strike me here. First, there is the plurality to the commands
given. It is not 'Hear, O parents' or 'Hear, O children's workers' but
'Hear, O Israel'. Today, parents are primarily responsible for raising
their children in the faith, but the whole community has a part to play.
The children of the church are 'our' children.

Second, there is a beauty to *how* we are to impress God's commands
on the next generation. We are to talk when at home, when away,
when we get up and when we lie down. Our task, whether or not we
have our own children, is to live out our faith and let 'our' children see
it in our daily lives.

Parenting for Faith

Through Parenting for Faith, BRF works to resource and empower parents, carers, and churches in raising children in the faith. We strive to
support as many as we can and give what we offer freely.

This is only possible because of generous donations from donors,
churches, charitable trusts, and gifts in wills.

We would love your support. You can find out more about Parenting
for Faith at **brf.org.uk/parentingforfaith**. If you can support this ministry financially, please consider whether you could give a regular gift.
You can find out how to give regularly via **brf.org.uk/friends** or get in
touch with us on **01235 462305** or via **giving@brf.org.uk**.

Your prayers, as ever, are hugely appreciated.

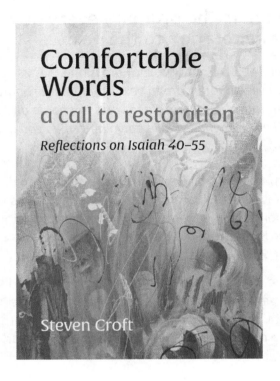

'Comfort, O comfort my people, says your God...' Through ten reflections, Steven Croft examines what these 'comfortable words' have to say to us. Each reflection begins from a passage of scripture taken from Isaiah 40—55: the song of an unnamed prophet who sings at the end of the exile to call God's people home. These are comfortable words the whole world needs to hear afresh in this season.

Comfortable Words: A Call to Restoration
Reflections on Isaiah 40—55
Steven Croft
978 1 80039 105 5 £7.99
brfonline.org.uk

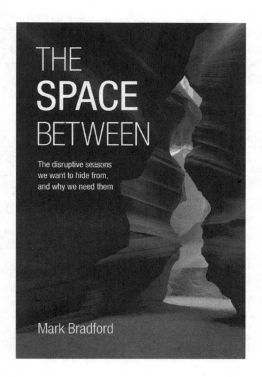

The disruptive seasons of life – those transition times in which we have left one season of stability but not yet arrived at the next – can be times of great disorientation. Yet, for good or for ill, they are also the most transformative. In *The Space Between*, Mark Bradford provides the reader with a biblical and theological understanding of such seasons of life, connects them with the resources to live faithfully through them and offers strength and hope for the journey.

The Space Between
The disruptive seasons we want to hide from, and why we need them
Mark Bradford
978 0 85746 825 3 £9.99
brfonline.org.uk

To order

Online: **brfonline.org.uk**
Telephone: +44 (0)1865 319700
Mon–Fri 9.30–17.00
Post: complete this form and send to the address below

Delivery times within the UK are normally 15 working days. Prices are correct at the time of going to press but may change without prior notice.

Title	Issue*	Price	Qty	Total
Messy Vintage		£8.99		
Comfortable Words		£7.99		
The Space Between		£9.99		
Bible Reflections for Older People (single copy)	Sep 21/Jan 22*	£5.25		

delete as appropriate

POSTAGE AND PACKING CHARGES			
Order value	UK	Europe	Rest of world
Under £7.00	£2.00		
£7.00–£29.99	£3.00	Available on request	Available on request
£30.00 and over	FREE		

Total value of books	
Donation*	
Postage and packing	
Total for this order	

Please complete in BLOCK CAPITALS

Title .... First name/initials .... Surname................................

Address ....

.... Postcode ....

Acc. No. .... Telephone ....

Email ....

Method of payment

❏ Cheque (made payable to BRF) ❏ MasterCard / Visa

Card no. ☐☐☐☐ ☐☐☐☐ ☐☐☐☐ ☐☐☐☐

Expires end ☐☐ ☐☐ Security code* ☐☐☐   Last 3 digits on the reverse of the card

Signature* .... Date .... / .... / ....

*ESSENTIAL IN ORDER TO PROCESS YOUR ORDER

Please return this form to:
BRF, 15 The Chambers, Vineyard, Abingdon OX14 3FE | enquiries@brf.org.uk
To read our terms and conditions, please visit **brfonline.org.uk/terms**.

BROP0221

The Bible Reading Fellowship (BRF) is a Registered Charity (233280)

BIBLE REFLECTIONS FOR OLDER PEOPLE **GROUP SUBSCRIPTION FORM**

> All our Bible reading notes can be ordered online
> by visiting **brfonline.org.uk/subscriptions**

The group subscription rate for *Bible Reflections for Older People* will be £15.75 per person until April 2022.

☐ I would like to take out a group subscription for .... (*quantity*) copies.
☐ Please start my order with the September 2021 / January 2022 / May 2022* issue.
    (*delete as appropriate*)

Please do not send any money with your order. Send your order to BRF and we will send you an invoice.

Name and address of the person organising the group subscription:

Title .... First name/initials .... Surname...

Address..

....Postcode ....

Telephone..................................... Email...

Church...

Name and address of the person paying the invoice if the invoice needs to be sent directly to them:

Title .... First name/initials .... Surname...

Address..

....Postcode ....

Telephone..................................... Email...

Please return this form to:
BRF, 15 The Chambers, Vineyard, Abingdon OX14 3FE | enquiries@brf.org.uk
To read our terms and conditions, please visit **brfonline.org.uk/terms**.

BROP0221

The Bible Reading Fellowship is a Registered Charity (233280)

BIBLE REFLECTIONS FOR OLDER PEOPLE **INDIVIDUAL/GIFT SUBSCRIPTION FORM**

To order online, please visit **brfonline.org.uk/subscriptions**

☐ I would like to take out a subscription (*complete your name and address details only once*)
☐ I would like to give a gift subscription (*please provide both names and addresses*)

Title .... First name/initials .... Surname ....

Address ....

.... Postcode ....

Telephone .... Email ....

Gift subscription name ....

Gift subscription address ....

.... Postcode ....

Gift message (*20 words max. or include your own gift card*):

....

....

Please send *Bible Reflections for Older People* beginning with the September 2021 / January 2022 / May 2022* issue (*delete as appropriate*):

(*please tick box*)	UK	Europe	Rest of world
Bible Reflections for Older People	☐ £19.95	☐ £27.45	☐ £31.50

Total enclosed £ .... (*cheques should be made payable to 'BRF'*)

Please charge my MasterCard / Visa ☐ Debit card ☐ with £ ....

Card no. ☐☐☐☐ ☐☐☐☐ ☐☐☐☐ ☐☐☐☐

Expires end ☐M☐M ☐Y☐Y Security code* ☐☐☐ Last 3 digits on the reverse of the card

Signature* _____ Date _____ / _____ / _____
*ESSENTIAL IN ORDER TO PROCESS YOUR ORDER

Please return this form to:
BRF, 15 The Chambers, Vineyard, Abingdon OX14 3FE | enquiries@brf.org.uk
To read our terms and conditions, please visit **brfonline.org.uk/terms**.

BROP0221

The Bible Reading Fellowship is a Registered Charity (233280)